W9-BWT-202

ANIMAL HANDLER:
12 THINGS TO KNOW

by Samantha S. Bell

STORY LIBRARY
MORE TO EXPLORE

www.12StoryLibrary.com

12-Story Library is an imprint of Bookstaves.

Developed and produced for 12-Story Library by Focus Strategic Communications Inc.

Library of Congress Cataloging-in-Publication Data
Cataloging-in-publication information is on file with the Library of Congress

ISBN
9781632359377 (hardcover)
9781632359728 (paperback)
9781645821021 (ebook)

Photographs ©: Jim Lambert/Shutterstock.com, cover, 1; spoonphol/Shutterstock.com, 4; JCVdude/YouTube.com, 4; Joe McDonald/Shutterstock.com, 5; Damien Maloney/History Channel/Everett Collection Inc./Alamy, 5; Nigmatulina Aleksandra/Shutterstock.com, 6; Jayme Burrows/Shutterstock.com, 7; CDC/Barbara Andrews, 7; Perla Sofia/Shutterstock.com, 8; Earthquest/Shutterstock.com, 9; Jay Ondreika/Shutterstock.com, 9; Stephen Barnes/Shutterstock.com, 10; Sari ONeal/Shutterstock.com, 11; Yammy8973/Shutterstock.com, 11; Africa Studio/Shutterstock.com, 12; John Roman Images/Shutterstock.com, 13; Dragosh Co/Shutterstock.com, 13; topimages/Shutterstock.com, 14; ABC News/YouTube.com, 15; DenisaPro/Shutterstock.com, 15; Catchlight Visual Services/Alamy, 16; Rudolph.A.furtado/CC1.0, 16; VGstockstudio/Shutterstock.com, 17; Sam Wordley/Shutterstock.com, 17; Paul Andrew Lawrence/Alamy, 18; Agung Wirantara/Shutterstock.com, 19; Richard Giles/CC3.0, 19; U.S. Navy/Brien Aho, 20; WaterFrame/Alamy, 21; Kyle Kittleson/YouTube.com, 21; mezzotint/Shutterstock.com, 22; Try my best/Shutterstock.com, 23; Dima Sidelnikov/Shutterstock.com, 23; Tommy Tortuga/CC4.0, 24; New Africa/Shutterstock.com, 25; Viktor Drachev/ITAR-TASS News Agency/Alamy, 25; kpzfoto/Alamy, 26; Africa Studio/Shutterstock.com, 27; Monkey Business Images/Shutterstock.com, 27; Michael Gäbler/CC3.0, 28; Ivonne Wierink/Shutterstock.com, 29; Marcel Jancovic/Shutterstock.com, 29

About the Cover

A zookeeper cares for a rhinoceros at the Denver Zoo.

Access free, up-to-date content on this topic plus a full digital version of this book. Scan the QR code on page 31 or use your school's login at 12StoryLibrary.com.

Table of Contents

1

Handling Venomous Animals Saves Lives

Some animal handlers work with venomous animals. They are often biologists with special training. They might work for a company or a zoo. Sometimes they work for themselves.

Some handlers are snake milkers. These people "milk" venom from a

7,500

Approximate number of people bitten by venomous snakes in the US each year

- About five people in the US die from snakebite each year.
- The snake milker positions the snake's fangs over a container or funnel.
- Yellow venom runs down the fangs. More powerful venom has a darker color.

snake's fangs. The venom is made into a freeze-dried powder. Sometimes it is used in medical research. It can be used to treat medical conditions, too. These include heart attacks and high blood pressure. The venom is also used to create the anti-venom. Anti-venom helps people who have been bitten by a poisonous snake.

DEADLY RESEARCH

Adam Thorn is a wildlife biologist. Rob Alleva is an animal handler. They wanted to learn more about venomous bites and stings. They allowed dangerous animals to bite or sting them. Then, they recorded how it affected them. They made their research into a reality television show, *Kings of Pain*.

Animal Handlers Face Health Risks

Dog bites are a risk of the job.

Many times when a person handles an animal, nothing will go wrong. But animals are unpredictable. They may become stressed if they are held down. They may try to kick, scratch, or bite.

Handlers are also at risk of catching certain diseases. Zoonosis is a disease that can be transmitted from an animal to a human. Handlers may also have to deal with allergic reactions to animal fur or feathers.

People who work with dogs also have to deal with the noise levels. Shelter and kennel workers often work with many dogs at one time. The noise level from barking dogs can cause hearing loss.

4.5 million

Approximate number of people in the US bitten by a dog each year

- Between 30 and 50 people die from dog bites each year in the US.
- Correct training can help animal handlers avoid injury.
- Handlers also wear protective gear such as bite suits to protect themselves.

A DEADLY BITE

Rabies is a disease that affects the nervous system of mammals. Rabies is spread when an infected animal bites another animal or a person. Rabies can be treated. But once the symptoms begin to show, the disease is fatal.

Wildlife Rehabilitators Help Injured Animals Get Home

Animals may become friendly with their rescuers.

Wildlife rehabilitators care for injured and sick wild animals. They also take care of orphaned animals. They feed the animals. They clean cages and dishes. They provide medical care with the help of a vet. When the animals are ready, the handlers release them back into the wild. Animals that wouldn't be able to survive in the wild may be used in educational programs.

Some rehabilitators specialize in working with certain types of animals. They may work with birds of prey, such as owls,

Condors can tell us about life in the wild.

hawks, and eagles. They may work with small mammals, such as rabbits and squirrels.

These handlers also educate people about the animals. They teach people how to handle situations that involve wildlife. They show people what to do if they find an injured animal. They help people understand how to act around wild animals.

THINK ABOUT IT

What wild animals have you seen in your neighborhood?

12

Number of hours rehabilitators work each day during the spring and summer

- People bring in lots of baby animals during the spring and summer.
- In the fall, they bring in young animals. Some become injured when they start out on their own.
- Handlers usually have less to do in the winter.

9

Big Animals Can Mean Big Danger

Even calm cows can injure handlers.

Some animal handlers work with large domesticated animals. They may work on a ranch with cattle. Some train horses for riding or show. They may work with donkeys or other farm animals. Some handlers work with llamas or camels. Handlers should start working with the animals when they are very young. This way, they will be easier to handle when they are grown.

These handlers must be careful because of the

A kick from a horse can cause injury.

animal's size. If a large animal attacks, the handler could be seriously injured or even killed. Bulls sometimes attack farm workers. Cows with calves may attack people, too. A person who works with these animals in fenced areas needs a plan for escape.

Even a trained horse can be dangerous. If a horse feels threatened, it will try to protect itself. It may try to run away. Or it may try to fight back by kicking or bucking.

3,000
Approximate number of camels in the US

- Camels have been used to carry people and supplies for hundreds of years.
- Some people work on camel farms.
- They milk the mother camels and sell the milk.

5

Police Officers Can Be Animal Handlers

German shepherds are a popular breed for police work.

Police dogs help police officers track criminals. They help them stop crimes. They help them find illegal substances, such as drugs or explosives. A police dog works with one handler. Since dogs are sometimes referred to as canines, the handler is called a K-9 officer. The officer must keep complete control of the dog at all times.

K-9 officers must know how to communicate with their dogs. They use basic hand signals as well as other commands. The officers and the dogs train together. They learn to trust each other.

To become a K-9 officer, a handler must have several years of experience as a police officer. Then, the officer can apply to join the K-9 unit. The officer is assigned a dog. Each officer continues to train their dog. The dogs live with the officers and their families. This way, they can bond better with the officers.

THINK ABOUT IT

Would you like to live with a police dog? Why or why not?

12 months
Age police dogs must be before beginning training

- Popular breeds for police dogs include German shepherds and Belgian Malinois.
- Bloodhounds help with search and rescue missions.
- Labrador retrievers are often used to find illegal substances.

Sensitive dog noses detect drugs or bombs.

6

Zoo Workers Take Care of Wild Animals

Huge animals can cause huge hurt.

Zookeepers take care of animals in zoos and wildlife preserves. They feed the animals. They make sure the animals get enough exercise. They keep the habitats in good condition.

Zoo veterinarians treat animals that are injured or sick. They also work to keep them healthy. They give

- In April 2019, a zookeeper in Kansas was attacked by a tiger.
- She was in the habitat to clean it, but the tiger was in there, too.
- The zookeeper survived. But she had bites on her head, neck, back, and arm.

vaccinations to prevent disease. They give the animals medicine if they do get sick. They clean teeth and perform surgery. They also decide the animals' diets and feeding schedules.

Some zoos keep track of every worker's location. The workers announce over a radio when they enter or leave certain areas. They carefully follow procedures. If they don't, some animals could injure or even kill the zoo worker.

DART

DART stands for Dangerous Animal Response Team. These teams are made up of zoo workers. They are highly trained sharpshooters. If possible, they use tranquilizer guns. They are always ready to protect people if an animal attacks.

15

7

Some Animal Handlers Work with Pets

Some animal handlers help people take care of their dogs, cats, and other pets. These animal handlers do many different kinds of jobs. Some work in kennels. A kennel is a place people take their pets when they go out of town. The kennel attendants take care of the pet while the owners are away. They clean the cages.

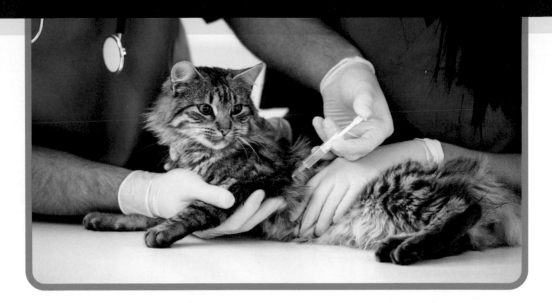

The attendants give the animals any medication they need.

Sometimes a person hires a pet sitter instead. The pet sitter takes care of the pets at the owner's home. Dog walkers take care of other people's dogs. They take them out every day to get exercise.

Veterinarians are animal doctors. They help pets that are sick or injured. They perform surgeries. They give the pets vaccinations. They give them medicine. They teach people how to care for their animals.

$69.5 billion
Amount of money spent on pets in the US in 2017

- Groomers keep pets looking nice.
- They wash dogs and cats and trim their fur and their nails.
- They might work in a pet shop, veterinary hospital, or animal shelter. Some run their own businesses.

Animal Control Officers Keep Animals and People Safe

Cities and states pass laws to regulate animals in areas where people live. Animal control officers are employed by a city or county government. They enforce the laws. This way, they help make sure both the animals and people are safe.

The officers handle all kinds of animals. This includes pets, farm animals, and wildlife. The officers receive information and complaints

Wild animals sometimes need to be protected.

about animals. They pick up stray animals and take them to shelters. They locate and capture dangerous animals. They help injured animals on the roads. They rescue trapped animals. They protect pets from abusive owners.

Rescued baby turtles.

800
Weight in pounds (363 kg) of a full-grown female moose

- In March 2019, a moose crashed through a toddler's bedroom window.
- Animal control officers came to get the moose out.
- The toddler and moose had a few cuts from the broken glass.

WRESTLING A REPTILE

Alligators and crocodiles are at home around lakes and rivers. But sometimes they wander into roadways and neighborhoods. Warmer temperatures can make them more active and aggressive. Handlers come to capture the reptiles. The handlers are known as wranglers. They return the animals to their natural habitats.

Steve Irwin was known as "The Crocodile Hunter."

Marine Mammal Handlers Work with Ocean Animals

The shows help people understand and respect sea life.

Some marine mammals are trained for military purposes. The US Navy trains bottlenose dolphins and California sea lions. The animals learn to find and recover objects that may be threats. These include mines and even spies.

The US Navy trained bottlenose dolphins to find lost equipment.

Marine mammal handlers train dolphins and whales. They also train seals and sea lions. Some animals perform in educational shows.

The trainers form bonds with the animals. They keep them healthy and happy. Many trainers join the International Marine Animal Trainers' Association (IMATA).

Handler with Beluga whales.

IMATA provides the trainers with opportunities to share ideas. It also offers training classes and support.

1959

Year the US Navy began training dolphins and sea lions

- Today, there are approximately 50 sea lions and 90 dolphins in the program.
- Most of the dolphins were bred by the Navy.
- Many of the sea lions came from rescue organizations.

AMERICA'S TEACHING ZOO

The Exotic Animal Training Management Program at Moorpark College in California accepts about 50 students per year. The students take care of nearly 200 animals at the college's zoo. Many people who finish the program go on to train dolphins and other marine mammals. Some even work in Hollywood.

10

Animal Handlers Need Training

Animal handlers train dogs.

Different jobs require different types of education. Most animal handlers need at least a high school diploma. Many handlers learn the skills they need by training on the job. They learn as they work. They may even shadow more experienced workers.

Marine mammal trainers don't need a college degree. But a degree is very helpful. Most trainers get degrees in areas such as marine biology or zoology, the science of animals. Some trainers have degrees from technical schools.

People who want to become vets need even more education. After graduating from college,

22

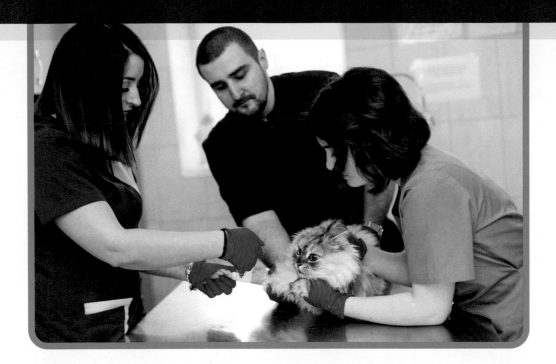

they go on to a veterinary school. The program last four years. Students study subjects such as animal body structure and behavior. They learn about animal health and diseases. They also get experience working with animals and their owners.

Handlers must like animals. They should learn to be patient. They must be compassionate toward the animals and their owners.

30
Number of veterinary schools in the US

- Students who want to be vets should start preparing in high school.
- They should take a lot of math and science classes.
- They can also volunteer at a clinic.

There Are Plenty of Jobs for Animal Handlers

Animal control officers capture and return escaped zoo animals.

There are different kinds of jobs for animal handlers. In many places, the number of jobs available is growing. Animal care and service workers take care of animals in kennels, pet stores, and vet clinics. The US Bureau of Labor Statistics predicts that these jobs will continue to increase through 2028. Caretakers earn approximately $24,000 a year.

Animal control officers enforce laws about animals. States with larger populations have more job opportunities. These include Texas and California. New York and Florida also have more jobs available. Animal control officers can make approximately $36,000 per year. They can work their way up to higher level positions.

Veterinarians provide medical care for animals. Veterinary technicians do the medical tests. Opportunities for these positions are growing, too.

In fact, the number of jobs for vets is increasing faster than jobs in other fields. Technicians earn approximately $34,000 a year. Veterinarians make approximately $94,000 a year.

330,900
Number of animal care and service jobs in 2018

- Some people own exotic pets, such as birds, snakes, and lizards.
- They also include mammals such as hedgehogs and pot-bellied pigs.
- They need special vets and other services for their pets.

Some Handlers Teach Animals to Help Others

Trainer in wheelchair with service dog.

Trainers may work with service animals, such as service dogs. Some people have disabilities. Service dogs are trained to help them perform certain tasks. Each dog is trained individually depending on what the person needs.

26 Trainers must understand the new owner's disability. That way, they will know how to train the dog. They help the dog and owner learn how to work together. They may travel to the owner's home to provide more training.

Some service dogs help people who are blind. Others may alert people with hearing loss about certain sounds.

Guide dogs are trained to help blind people.

Others might help people in wheelchairs by opening doors or cabinets. They may help them reach things. Medical alert dogs watch for medical issues such as seizures or low blood sugar.

THINK ABOUT IT

You should not pat a service dog. The dog might get distracted. Think about a time you were distracted in school. How did you do?

500,000

Approximate number of service dogs in the US

- Some dogs are trained as therapy dogs.
- They go with their owners to hospitals, schools, and nursing homes.
- They provide comfort and affection to many different people.

More Daring and Dangerous Jobs

Beekeeper

Beekeepers make sure their beehives are healthy. They also collect products to sell. These include honey and honeycomb. The honeycomb is made into beeswax. The wax is used in makeup and soap.

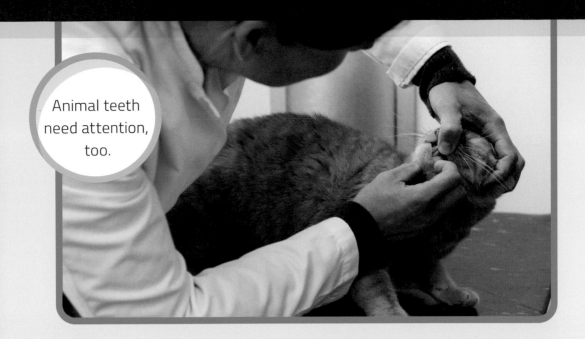

Animal teeth need attention, too.

Laboratory Animal Worker

Laboratory animal workers work in labs. The lab workers feed and care for the animals in the lab. They help animal scientists and veterinarians.

Animal Dentist

Animal dentists are veterinarians. They must have extra training to learn how to work on animal teeth. They can clean, pull, or repair animal teeth.

Police dog trainers wear protective pads.

Police Dog Trainer

Police dog trainers choose the dogs they think will work well with a police unit. Then they teach the dogs how to follow commands. Sometimes the trainer is also the handler. Other times, the trainer works for a private company.

29

Glossary

abuse
Harsh or cruel treatment of animals.

compassionate
Showing kindness or concern for another living thing.

domesticated
Tamed and kept in a home or on a farm.

exotic
A species of animal that comes from another country.

fatal
Causing death, such as diseases like rabies.

regulate
To control something by rules, such as by laws about the treatment of animals.

rehabilitation
Treatment to help an animal regain its health and strength after injury or illness.

shadow
To follow and observe someone closely to see how they do their job.

unpredictable
Behaving in a way that is unexpected so that it is impossible to know what will happen.

vaccination
Treatment that makes an animal resistant to a certain disease.

venomous
Poisonous, such as the bites of certain spiders and snakes.

Read More

Bedell, J.M. *So, You Want to Work with Animals?* New York, NY: Simon & Schuster, Aladdin Books, 2017.

George, Michael. *Life at the Zoo.* New York, NY: Sterling, 2018.

Hestermann, Josh, and Bethanie Hestermann. *Zoology for Kids: Understanding and Working with Animals, with 21 Activities.* Chicago, IL: Chicago Review Press, 2015.

Visit 12StoryLibrary.com

Scan the code or use your school's login at **12StoryLibrary.com** for recent updates about this topic and a full digital version of this book. Enjoy free access to:

- Digital ebook
- Breaking news updates
- Live content feeds
- Videos, interactive maps, and graphics
- Additional web resources

Note to educators: Visit 12StoryLibrary.com/register to sign up for free premium website access. Enjoy live content plus a full digital version of every 12-Story Library book you own for every student at your school.

Index

About the Author

Samantha S. Bell has written more than 125 nonfiction books for children. She also teaches art and creative writing to children and adults. She lives in the Carolinas with her family and too many cats.